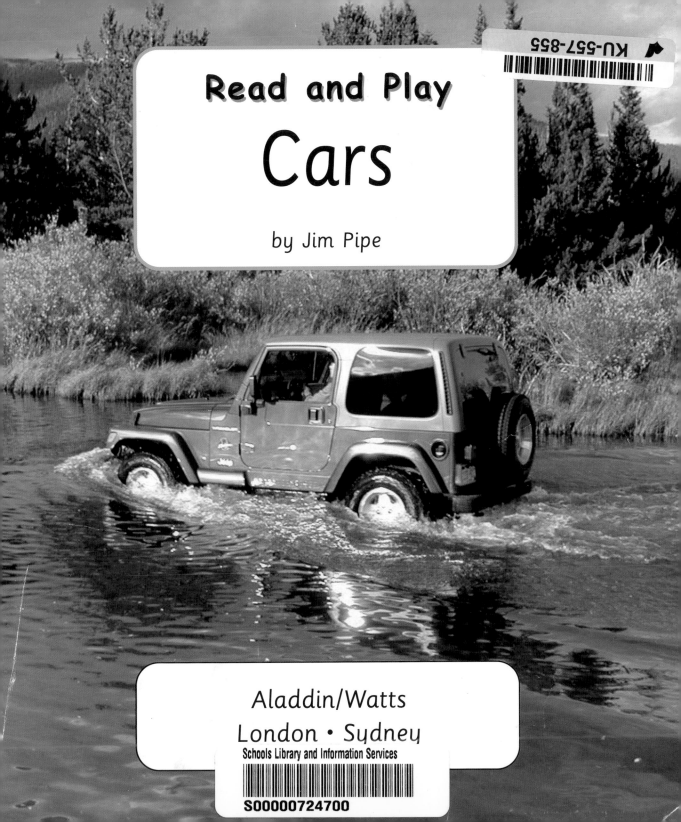

Read and Play
Cars

by Jim Pipe

Aladdin/Watts

London • Sydney

car

2

This is a **car**.

A **car** carries people.

3

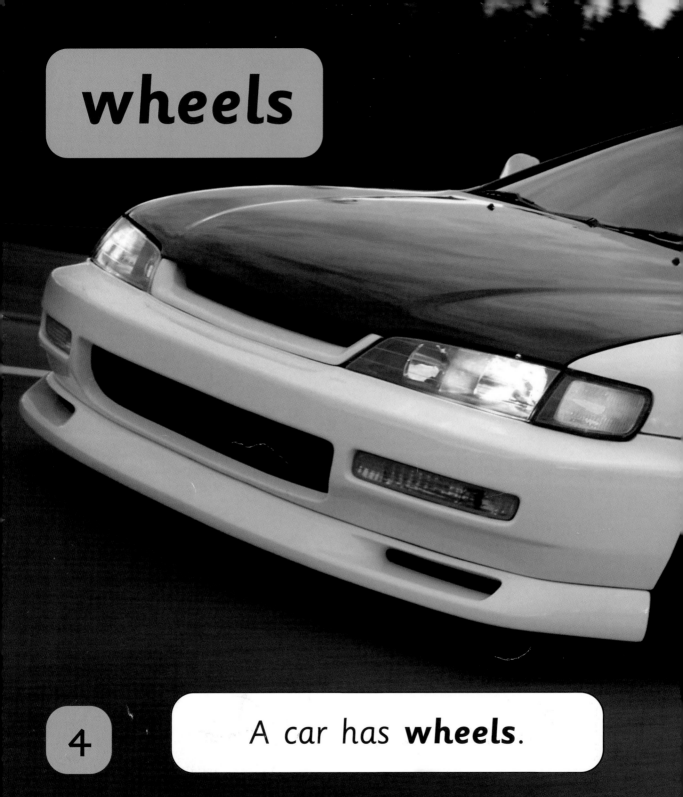

wheels

4

A car has **wheels**.

This car has four **wheels**.

5

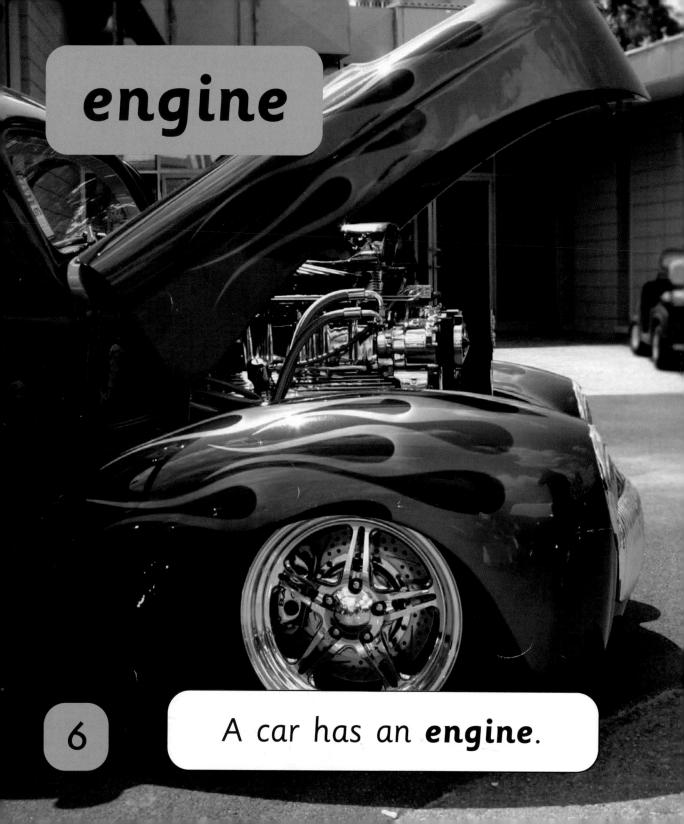

engine

6

A car has an **engine**.

fuel

An engine needs **fuel**.

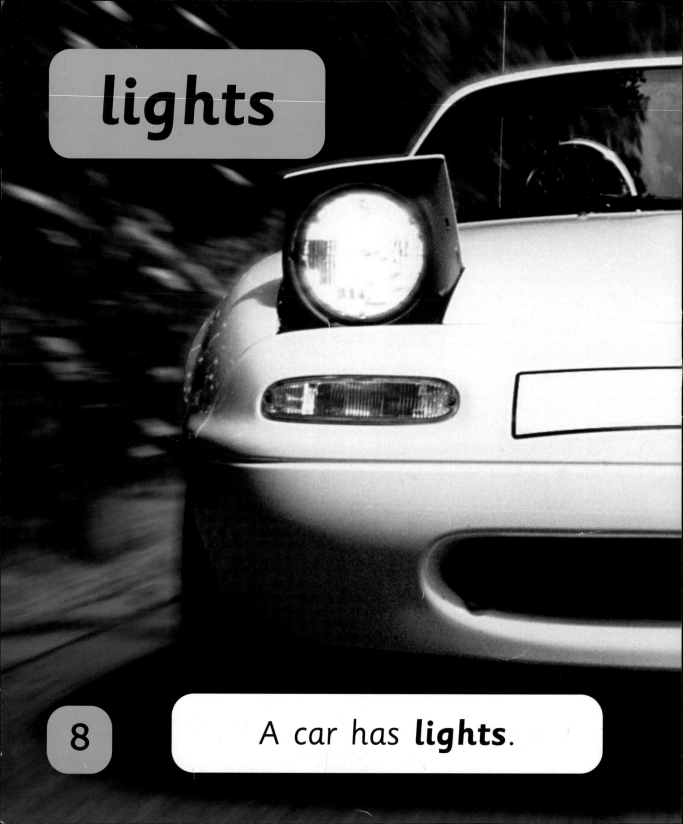

lights

A car has **lights**.

Lights shine on the road.

9

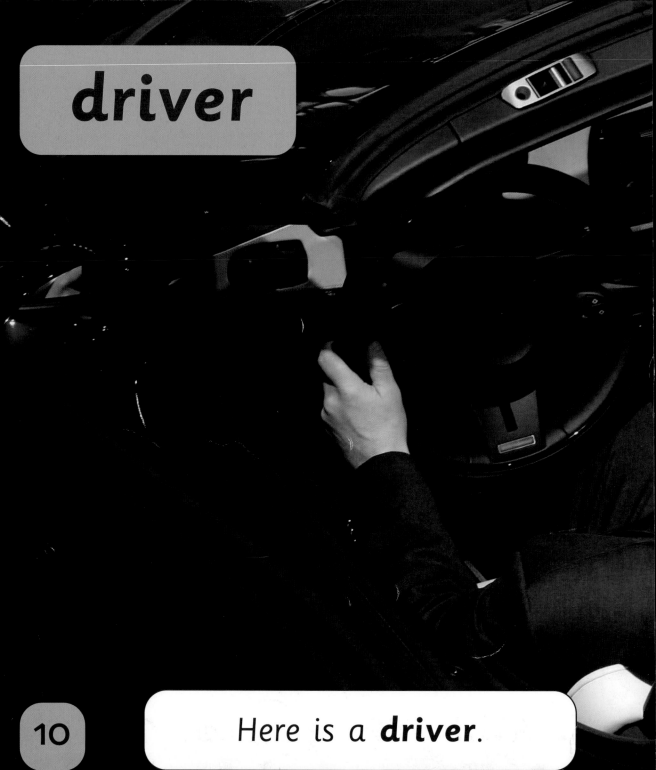

driver

Here is a **driver**.

A **driver** drives the car.

11

road

This car is on the **road**.

12

This car is off the **road.**

13

tyre

14

This is a **tyre.**

A **tyre** grips the road.

15

racing

16

This is a **racing** car.

It goes very fast.

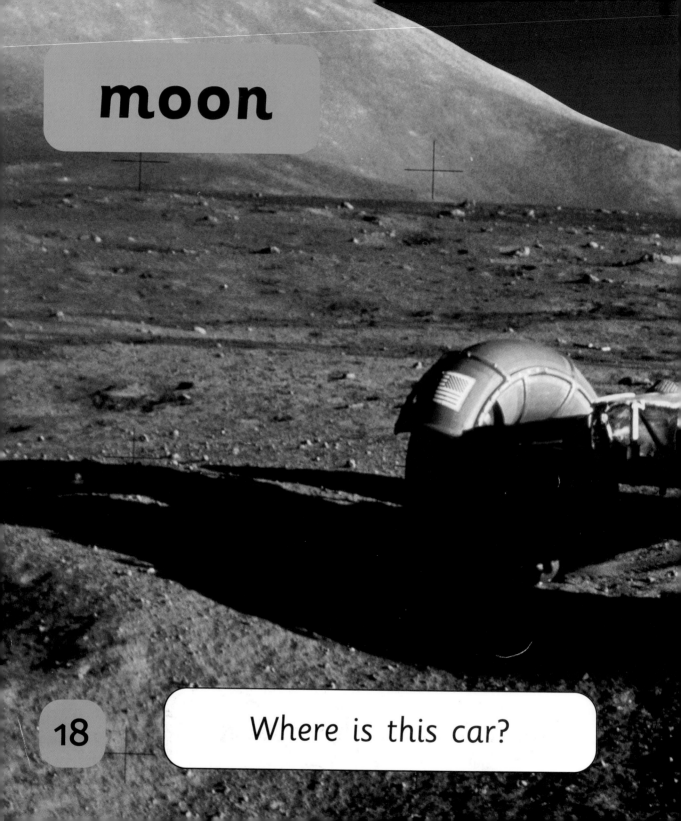

moon

18

Where is this car?

This car is on the **moon**.

19

What am I?

light

wheel

fuel

tyre

Match the words and pictures.

How many?

Can you count the red cars?

What noise?

Brm! Brm!

Screech!

Wee-oh!

Beep! Beep!

Can you make car noises?

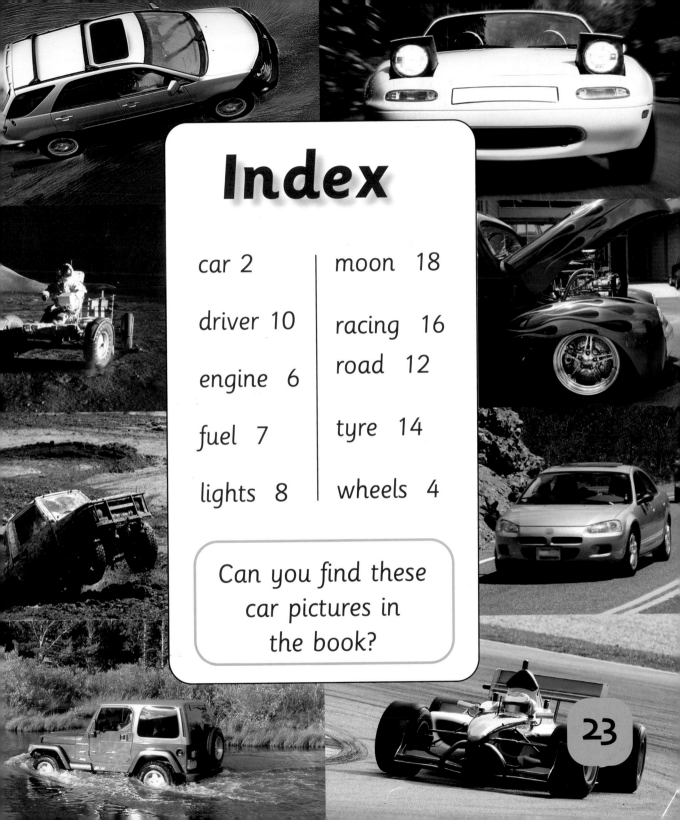

Index

Can you find these
car pictures in
the book?

23

For Parents and Teachers

Questions you could ask:

p. 2 Where do you think they are going? Encourage reader to think about long and short journeys, e.g. going to school/work/shops, visiting family/friends.

p. 4 What shape are wheels? Round/circles. Ask reader if they think wheels would work as well if they were shaped like squares/triangles etc.

p. 7 Where do you fill up a car? At a garage/petrol pump. An engine needs fuel to work. Ask what happens when a car runs out of fuel.

p. 9 When does a driver turn on the lights? At night or when it is foggy/rainy. Lights also warn other drivers, e.g. brake lights, indicators.

p.10 How does a driver turn the car left or right? By turning the steering wheel. You could also describe controls used to slow down and speed up.

p. 12 Why do cars drive on roads? A road is hard and smooth. Driving off road is bumpy/muddy.

p. 14 What other machines have tyres? e.g. bicycles, trucks, tractors – but not trains.

p.16 What shape is this car? Low/flat/smooth. Compare this shape with other cars in the book.

p.18 Who is driving this car? Astronaut. The car, called a buggy, was taken to the moon by a rocket.

Activities you could do:

• Ask the reader to describe a long or short journey they have made in a car. Ask them to compare time taken to walk somewhere or go in a car.

• Look at patterns made by wheeled toy cars as they are pushed through wet sand, over dough etc. Compare with tyre marks made by bicycles.

• Role play: encourage reader to imagine themselves driving a car, e.g. starting using keys, steering wheel, stopping and going faster.

• Compare toy cars/car pictures in magazines, looking at different types of vehicles, e.g. family cars, racing cars, vans, sports cars and jeeps.

• Encourage the reader to draw a car, writing labels for wheels, driver etc.

Paperback Edition 2009
© **Aladdin Books Ltd 2006**
All rights reserved
Designed and produced by
Aladdin Books Ltd
PO Box 53987
London SW15 2SF

First published in 2006
by Franklin Watts
338 Euston Road
London NW1 3BH

Franklin Watts Australia
Level 17/207 Kent Street
Sydney NSW 2000

Franklin Watts is a division of Hachette Children's Books, an Hachette Livre company.
www.hachettelivre.co.uk

ISBN 978 0 7496 8973 5

A catalogue record for this book is available from the British Library.

Dewey Classification: 629.222

Printed in Malaysia

Series consultant
Zoe Stillwell is an experienced Early Years teacher currently teaching at Pewley Down Infant School, Guildford.

Photocredits:
l-left, t-top, m-middle
All photos from istockphoto.com except: 18-19, 23mtl — NASA.